The Hoax That is Still Alive

The Protocols of the Elders of Zion

Ian Day

DEDICATION

My first paperback is dedicated to my wife, two children, and the three cats
we have at Ranch Diablo, our home in Arizona.

Table of Contents

ACKNOWLEDGMENTS

Ian Day would like to thank Cliff Caswell of Abrandax Publishing for helping to release these writings.

"Cliff, you have changed my life."

1 The Big Lie vs Reality

The Protocols of the Elders of Zion are a mysterious series of documents that outline a Jewish Conspiracy to take out the world.

Nineteenth century Russia's Tsarist police created the Protocols to take the heat off the Romanov family's ineffectual government, they encourage anti-Semitism, and paint potential revolutionaries as tools of the alleged Jewish Conspiracy.

2 Jewish Conspiracy

The Protocols of the Learned Elders of Zion was designed to take the heat off the Romanov family's inefficacious governance of Russia by creating the troublemakers for a political change as followers of a Jewish Conspiracy to rule the world.

It was used as a false doctrine to incite pogroms against Russia's Jewish communities.

When many anti-Communist White Russians fled Russia in the years following the Bolshevik Revolution of 1917, Russia's particular brand of anti-Semitism traveled with them and The Protocol began to be translated into the languages of Western Europe and beyond.

One of the most notable supporters included car industry Henry Ford. However, their most detrimental use was as a philosophical underpinning for Adolf Hitler's MEIN KAMPF, which spread to the persecution of the Jews in Germany and culminated in the genocidal reality of the Final Solution.

The Protocols' influence on Hitler's Nazi philosophy was such that some have called the document "a warrant for global genocide." Although known to be a lie in Russia from the outset and publicity outed as fraudulent in the 1920s, anti-Semitic groups the world over continued to publish The Protocols.

Even to this day, The Protocols are frequently used to incite religious hatred and millions of people still believe in it, from radical ultra-right-wing groups to American Christian extremist sects to fundamental Islamists. In some Middle Eastern countries, they can even be found on the school syllabus. They are clearly a lie that won't die.

3 Creating the Big Lie

The Protocols of the Elders of Zion consist of twenty-four protocols alleged to be the written record of a cloistered gathering of a group of the world's highest ranking Jewish leaders toward the end of the nineteenth century at which they made plans to achieve world domination.

The number of the Elders of Zion is said to be 300 men and their text is positioned as sacred advice from the presiding Elders to current and future Jewish initiates.

Each of the twenty-four protocols (see outline: "The Twenty-four Protocols" at the end of this commentary for the list) is divided into a series of aphorisms that discuss tactics for taking over a world defined by goyim-- the Yiddish word for a non-Jew--laxity, and decadence.

The plan is to use the weakness of goyim against themselves.

The socialist movements sweeping Europe in the eighteenth and nineteenth centuries are presented as a plot the Jews have hatched to kill off the non-Jewish population.

"We appear on the scene as the saviors of the workers from this oppression when we proposed to him to enter the ranks of our fighting forces--socialists, anarchists, communists--to whom we always give support in accordance with a brotherly rule (of solidarity of all humanity) of our social masonry.

The aristocracy, which enjoyed by law the labor of the workers, was interested in seeing that the workers were well fed, healthy and strong.

We are interested in just the opposite--in the diminution, the killing out of the goyim.

Our power is in the chronic shortness of food and physical weakness of the worker because by all that this implies that he is made the slave of our will, and he will not find in his own authorities either strength or energy to set against our will.

Hunger creates the right of capital to rule the worker more surely that it was given to the aristocracy by the legal authority of king."

In this representation the liberals and revolutionaries who are fighting to over-throw governments in apparent interest of the people are recast as mere pawns of the Elders of Zion, who will usurp them once the old order has been dispatched with. There are sections that deal with the financial systems of the world, usually the cornerstone for those interested in peddling Jewish conspiracies, while other sections evoke other famous anti-Semitic myths such as the blood libel whereby Jews were accused of using the fresh blood of Christian children in their Passover feasts.

4 Russian Beginnings

The Protocols first appeared publicly in a right-wing St. Petersburg newspaper, Znamya (the banner), in serial form between August 28 and September 7, 1903.

The editor and publisher, Pavel Krushevan, was a member of the Black Hundredists, a group of anti-Semitic, ultra-nationalist right-wingers who were working to preserve the authority of the Orthodox Church and the tsar.

Four months prior to their publication, another Krushevan newspaper, Besserabetz, had helped incite a pogrom against the Jews in Kishinev (now Chisinau, the capital of Moldavia), where 49 Jews were killed, more than 500 injured, and 700 houses and stores destroyed.

5 German Connection

In 1868, a German novelist named Hermann Goedsche, using English pen name Sir John Retcliffe, published a novel titled Biarritz.

The plot centered on a Jewish cabal intent on taking over the world. Goedsche appears to have been inspired by the French writer Maurice Joly, whose Dialogues in Hell Between Machiavelli and Montesquieu a publication based on opposition to Napoleon III.

Goedsche, a notorious anti-Semite, lifted Joly's plot device, introducing Jews to the story line as the villains.

Near the end of the nineteenth century Russian czar Nicolas II in a move designed to strengthen his hand among the Russian people and weaken his political opponents, the czar demanded a device that would expose his enemies as allies in a conspiracy involving world domination.

With the czar's directive, the Russian Okhrana secret police force plundered various sources for inspiration.

They found it in Goedsche's novel, and in 1897 published as fact the section dealing with the Jewish plot.

Eight years later, the Protocols were translated into English and widely circulated as minutes recorded during the First Zionist Congress held in Basel, Switzerland, in 1897 presided over by "the Father of Modern Zionism," Theodor Herzl.

The Protocols are intended to be read like an instruction manual for running the world. Assisting in the ambitious project of global domination, the documents declared, are the Freemason, whose agenda is being manipulated by the Elders, and the Bavarian Illuminate, who are either dupes or willing participants.

6 Great Within the Small

The Protocols were subsequently published in full in the year 1905, as the final chapter to religious fanatic Sergei Nilus' apocalyptic tome THE GREAT WITHIN THE SMALL: Antichrist Considered as an Imminent Political Possibility, Notes of an Orthodox Believer.

Nilus saw the world in religious terms.

For him, the socialist's revolution was analogous to the predictions in the Bible's Book of Revelation that before the second coming of Christ, the anti-Christ would come, be celebrated by the Jews as the Messiah, and take over the world.

He claimed to have seen secret documents whereby King Solomon the Wise, as long ago as 929 B.C., had met with his council of elders at the citadel in Jerusalem to develop a plan to conquer the world without bloodshed.

Over the intervening centuries, this plan had been fine-tuned by successive generations of Jewish Elders to the point where it was now on the cusp (according to Nilus) of being successfully implemented.

The copy of The Protocols he was publishing, he further claimed, had been stolen from the Jewish Elders and given to him by an anonymous source.

7 The Evolution of the Fraud

A lawyer and mystic, Sergei Nilus profited from the superstitions and intrigues of the Russian court toward the turn of the Twentieth century.

His wife had influence with the Tsarina and her sister, and it was through this that Nilus got permission to publish The Protocols, overturning the previous ban of them by Nicolas II.

Over numerous subsequent editions, his story of how he came to get his hands on them changed on more than one occasion.

In the 1911 edition introduction to his book, Nilus wrote:

"In 1901, I succeeded through an acquaintance of mine (the late Court Marshal Alexei Nicolayevitch Sukotin of Tchernigov) in getting a manuscript that exposed with unusual perfection and clarity the course and development of the clandestine Jewish who gave me this manuscript guaranteed it to be a faithful translation of the original documents that were stolen by an enterprising young woman from one of the highest and most influential leaders of the Freemason at an exclusive meeting somewhere in France--the beloved nest of Freemasonic conspiracy."

Yet in his 1905 edition, Nilus claimed that The Protocols had been written at a meeting of the Elders of Zion held in 1902-03. By the time of his 1917 edition, the source had changed again.

This time it was allegedly the first Zionist conference, which took place in 1897 at Basel, Switzerland. He claimed it was Circular 19 of the conference. Yet this document was never found, and it is highly unlikely it ever existed.

In an epilogue to the first English edition published in 1920, Nilus changed his mind again, claiming that "My friend found them in the safes at the headquarters of the Society of Zion, which are at present situated in France."

8 A Diversion From Incompetence

It might seem ludicrous that such a poorly verified work from a second-rate pseudo-philosopher should gain any significant traction on Russia's political debate.

However, Russia at the time was a ludicrous place.

Both the tsar and his wife were heavily under the influence of mystics and charismatic charlatans such as Rasputin.

Tsar Nicholas had adopted his father's autocratic persona but lacked the intellectual capacity to rule effectively, leaving him susceptible both to views of religious fanatics such as Nilus, who romanticized the tsar, as well as to more able ultra-national forces as the Black Hundredists.

Like his father, Alexander III, Nicolas was a committed anti-Semite.

The Protocols were introduced into the royal household by Grand Prince Sergei Alexandrovich, who was also governor of Moscow, had close connections to the Black Hundredists, and was personally involved in discrimination against the Jews.

Not only was Sergei the uncle of the tsar, but he was also married to Elizaveta, the sister of the tsarina, Alexandra.

It's not known exactly when Nicolas got to read The Protocols, though it preceded their publication. His initial reaction was enthusiastic.

They were a pleasant, casual diversion from the effects of his own incompetence and helped to confirm his belief that "everywhere one can recognize the directing and destroying hand of Judaism."

Like Adolf Hitler, he was planning on incorporating The Protocols as a linchpin of his politics.

However, his interior minister, Pyotr Stolypin, had several people investigate The Protocols to see whether they could be deployed as the foundation for a major anti-Semitic campaign, only to discover they were a fraud.

In response to hearing this, Nicolas, who, although incompetent, maintained a sense of honor, ordered "Drop The Protocols! One cannot defend a pure cause by dirty methods."

Consequently, The Protocols were banned.

To sum up: The last Russian tsar Nicolas II, who was killed by the Bolsheviks during the Russian Revolution, to deflect from his own problems, the Russian Government encouraged anti-Semitic conspiracy theories.

When he first read The Protocols, he was enthusiastic.

However, on discovering that they were most likely a fraud, his sense of honor prevailed and prevented him from allowing them to be used officially to stir up anti-Semitic sentiment and rhetoric.

9 The Publication of the Protocols

Just because the tsar had washed his hands of this questionable document didn't mean it was finished.

Many in the ultra-nationalistic side of politics were concerned about the tsar's ability to resist the tide of Liberalism, while politicians such as Stolypin, who proposed to stabilize Russian society by creating a class of wealthy peasants, were perceived by the left and right alike as a danger to their agendas.

Princess Elizaveta was concerned about a cooling in the relationships between her tsarina sister and herself.

One of the reasons for this she thought was the influence French occultist and hypnotists Pierre Vachet had at court. Elizaveta contrived to have the French man replaced with a more Russian mystic.

Her thoughts turned to Sergei Nilus.

The attempt was not successful, yet in introducing Nilus to the court, Elizaveta managed to get him married to one of the tsarina's ladies-in-waiting.

Elena Ozeroa, whose uncle, Philip Stepanov, had first introduced The Protocols to Grand Prince Sergei.

On behalf of her husband Nilus who, although qualified as a lawyer, was not too much of a mystic to make much of a living of it.

Ozeroa petitioned the government's censorship committee to overturn the ban on The Protocols, so her husband could use them in his book.

Against the backdrop of the chaotic 1905 Revolution (which saw the assassination of Grand Prince Sergei, who was known for his ultra-conservatism and cruelty), Nilus received permission to publish The Protocols in September of 1905.

Given that every edition and translation in the world can be traced back to this edition, it was the moment when the future of one of history's greatest lies   became   assured.

10 The Lie Spreads to Western Europe

As the political crisis in Russia developed into the Bolshevik Revolution of 1917, the ultra-nationalists increasingly tried to garner the support of the peasants by associating the Bolshevik revolutionaries with a Jewish conspiracy to rule the world.

They were helped in this by the fact that there were quite a few Jewish Bolshviks, most notably revolutionary leader, Leon Trotsky.

As the Red Army gained ascendancy in the Revolution, many White Russians fled to Europe and America.

For many of these displaced Russians who had lost their land, social status, and possessions, the 1917 Revolution was proof that The Protocols were true.

Some took copies of Nilus' text containing The Protocols with them, and it was from these that The Protocols came to be translated into other European languages.

The association of the Bolshevik Revolution with a Jewish conspiracy peddled by the White Russians caught the attention of anti-Semites all over the world.

Interestingly, in the first English language edition, published in the Philadelphia Public Ledger by journalist Carl Ackerman, make references to the Bolsheviks.

The first explicitly anti-Semitic English language edition appeared in Britain in the Morning Post in the year 1920.

It was followed with an anonymous translation titled The Jewish Peril by a racist publishing outfit, the Britons, in the same year. Other editions were not long in coming to be.

Perhaps the most powerful man to grab on to The Protocols and run with them was Henry Ford, who purchased the Dearborn Independent paper primarily as a vehicle for exercising his anti-Semitic beliefs.

Whereas many people identified the Jewish Peril with the Bolsheviks, others in America such as Ford were concerned with the perceived Jewish hegemony over the finance industry worldwide and the emerging motion picture business in Hollywood, California.

The great thing about The Protocols, at least for the conspiracy minded anti-Semites, was that it provided a theory that could be deployed against the perceived influence of Jews whether they were left or right wing, pillars of society or revolutionaries.

11 Literary Fabrication

As The Protocols spread into the major European languages and were read by millions, evidence increasingly began to build that they were a fraud.

Nilus was probably enough of a zealot to believe the story he was being fed was the truth.

Yet as Nicolas' initial decision not to permit the publication of The Protocols showed, there were many in Russia who believed them to be a fraud from the outset.

However, the extent of the fraud only became apparent as translations proliferated and more and more people became curious as to the origins of this strange document.

Perhaps the breakthrough came in 1921, when the Constantinople correspondent for the English Times, Phillip Graves, was approached by a Russian emigre in dire financial straits with a manuscript.

Although the title page was missing, it had been printed in Geneva in 1864. Graves wrote in the Times:

"Before receiving the book from Mr. X, I was, as I have said, incredulous. I did not believe that Sergei Nilus' Protocols wre authentic; they explained too much by theory of a vast Jewish conspiracy. Professor Nilus' account of how they were obtained was too melodramatic to be credible, and it was hard to believe that real 'Learned Elders of Zion' would not have produced a more intelligent political scheme than the crude and theatrical subtitles of The Protocols. But I could not have believed, had I not seen, that the writer who supplied Nilus with his originals was a careless and shameless plagiarist."

Unbeknownst to him, Graves had been given by his Mr. X a copy of a pamphlet that had been written in French by Marice Joly to satirize the ambition of France's Louis Napoleon, the ambitious, authoritarian, and ultimately disastrous nephew of Napoleon who ruled France from 1852-1870.

On the missing title page was Dialogue aux enfers entre Machiavel et Montesquieu (A Dialogue in Hell Between Machiavelli and Montesquieu).

In the text the two philosophers meet on a deserted beach in hell and enjoy a Socratic dialogue. Montesquieu, the French essayist and enlightenment philosopher, advocates the liberal cause while Machiavelli is there as a thinly disgused references to the Hausmannisation of Paris, which saw many of the old neighborhoods of Paris demolished to make way for the grand boulevards today, Louis Napoleon's financial extravagance, and his use of secret societies as an agent of foreign policy.

Joly was arrested and jailed when he tried to smuggle copies of the pamphlet into France and eventually committed suicide in 1879. He could never have imagined that he would have posthumously become the author of large chunks of The Protocols of Zion. Although the French police destroyed most of the copies of his Geneva Dialogues, one surviving copy found its way into the hands of the Tsarist Secret Service, the Okhrana, in Geneva. Grave's article showed that entire slabs of Joly's book has been translated into Russian and then copied into The Protocols.

FOR EXAMPLE:
"You do not know the unbounded meanness of peoples...groveling before force, pitiless toward the weak, implacable to faults, indulgent to crimes, incapable of supporting the contradictions of a free regime, and patient to the point of martyrdom under the violence of an audacious despotism...giving themselves masters whom they pardon for deeds for the least of which they would have beheaded twenty constitutional kings."
--Machiavelli, in The Geneva Dialogues, p. 43

COMPARED TO:

"In their intense meanness the Christians peoples help our independence--
when kneeling they crouch before power; when they are pitiless toward the
weak; merciless in dealing with faults, lenient to crimes; when they refuse to
recognize the contradictions of freedom, when they are patient to the
degree of martyrdom in bearing with the violence of an audacious
despotism. At the hands of their present dictators, Premiers, and ministers,
they endure abuses for the smallest of which they would have murdered
twenty kings."
--The Protocols of the Elders of Zion, p. 15

The Geneva Dialogues was not the only text used in the creation of The
Protocols. The idea of a meeting of the Elders of Zion has been traced to a
novel called Biarritz by Sir John Retcliffe. Retcliffe was not a Sir at all.
Rather he was Hermann Goedsche, a Prussian postal worker and
reactionary who was fired from the Prussian postal service for forging-
letters implicating the democratic leader, Benedic Waldeck, in a plot against
the Prussian regime. Finding himself without an income, Goedsche began
to write sensationalist romance novels. He was also an avowed anti-Semite.
Biarritz was published in 1868. In one chapter, "At the Jewish Cemetery at
Prague," Goedsche, ignorant of the fact that the ten of the twelve tribes of
Israel no longer existed, wrote a scene where the twelve Jewish leaders meet
Satan in a graveyard, report on the status of their conspiracy toward world
domination, and come away with the intention of being Kings of the world
within the century.

Many of the strategies discussed to achieve this domination seem to have
been copied directly from Joly's Dialogues.

Given that the Jewish Cemetery chapter of Goedsche's novel was translated
into Russian and circulated independently as a pamphlet, it's quite likely it
was the catalyst for the eventual fusing of the two texts in The Protocols.

12 Author Still Unknown

So, if it wasn't the Elders of Zion who wrote the document, the who wrote it?

It remains uncertain as to exactly who wrote The Protocols, but it's likely the fraud was created at the direction of the Paris head of the Okhrana at the time, Pyotr Rachovsky, to try and link the opponents of the tsar to a worldwide Jewish conspiracy.

The man most identified with its writing is Mathieu Golovinski, a Russian aristocrat whose father had been a friend of novelist Fyodor Dostoevsky. At university, Golovinski joined the Holy Brotherhood, an ultra-nationalist, anti-Semitic secret society that used forged documents to discredit revolutionaries.

From there he went to work for the tsar's government press department as a spin doctor and briber of journalists.

Eventually, his scheming got the better of him, and he was denounced as an informer by novelist Maxim Gorky and dismissed.

Golovinski became a freelancer of sorts and worked with the son of Maurice Joly at a Paris newspaper, where he probably discovered the Geneva Dialogues.

He was hired by Rachovsky to write The Protocols as a piece of propaganda.

Showing himself to be a man of intrigue and opportunism rather than ideals, Golovinski went on to scheme for the Bolsheviks after the 1917 Revolution until his death in 1920.

It was during this same period that his fraud began to extend its influence in the world.

13 Significance of the Hoax

To what extent the whole existence of this people is based on a continuous lie is shown incomparably by The Protocols of the Wise Men of Zion, so infinitely hated by the Jews.

They are based on a forgery, the Frankfurter Zeitung moans and screams once a week: the best proof that they are authentic.

What many Jews may do unconsciously is here consciously exposed. And that is what matters.

Mein Kampf was written while Hitler was in prison and published in 1926.

Mein Kampf was a bombastic amalgam of autobiography and political philosophy.

Its anti-Semitism leaned heavily on a fervent belief in the Protocols of the Elders of Zion.

"It is completely indifferent from what Jewish brain these disclosures originate; the important thing is that with positively terrifying certainty they reveal the nature and activity of the Jewish people and expose their inner contexts as well as their final aims. The best criticism applied to them, however, is reality. Anyone who examines the historical development of the last hundred years from the standpoint of this book has become the common property of a people, the Jewish menace may be considered as broken." --Mein Kampf by Adolf Hitler

More than anything else, the significance of The Protocols can be found in Hitler's use of them as a foundation for his Anti-Semitism.

The devastation caused to Germany by the conditions of surrender under the Treaty of Versailles created conditions extremely conducive for conspiracy theory.

The Protocols emerged as just the right time and immediately found an eager German audience.

Although books and articles had shown The Protocols to be a lie at least since 1920, Hitler, as have many since, had no trouble in asserting them as truth.

Although it's unlikely that the absence of The Protocols would have prevented the ascendancy of Hitler and his rabid anti-Semitism, they were useful, and as such can be considered a contributing factor to the rise of the Nazis, and the Final Solution.

14 Henry Ford

Other notable adherents to The Protocols of that era included car maker and political crank, Henry Ford, was an avowed anti-Semite, and even bought a newspaper, The Dearborn Independent, primarily for the purposes of expounding his anti-Semitic views.

He was one of the strongest advocates of the truth of The Protocols of the Elders of Zion.

When he was eventually forced to recognize that The Protocols were a fraud, he claimed unconvincingly that his staff had misled him.

In a statement Ford said:

"The only statement I care to make about The Protocols is that they fit in with what is going on. They are sixteen years old now, and they have fitted the world situation up to this time. They fit now."

Despite all the evidence to the contrary, Ford maintained the truth of The Protocols until 1927, when he was forced to make a public recantation, which he did by passing the buck onto his staff, arguing unconvincingly that they had mislead him into believing their authenticity.

Given Ford's central role in the American military-industrial complex and his admiration of Hitler, it's possible The Protocols played a small part in the political atmosphere that caused the United States' tardy entry into World War II.

One could be forgiven for thinking that after the Holocaust, The Protocols would have been consigned to history as one of the world's ugliest lies.

Yet they have continued to prosper, particularly in the Middle East, where they help fuel the long-running conflicts between the Israelis and the Arab world.

In some countries such as Saudi Arabia, The Protocols can even be found on school syllabuses.

The oppressive ruling elites of these countries see the same opportunity that Tsar Nicolas did: The Protocols are a convenient way of finding scapegoats for the poor living conditions most inhabitants of the Arab world continue to live in.

Paradoxically, one of the other major proponents of The Protocols as truth tend to be conservative Christian groups.

The rise of Neo-Nazism, particularly among the many disaffected people of the former Soviet bloc, is another place where The Protocols are enjoying a resurgence in the hands of people who could care less about the authenticity of the lies.

15 Practical Lessons of the Protocols

Protocol No. 1, for example, "Therefore, in governing the world the best results are obtained by violence and intimidation, and not by academic discussions," while Protocol No. 23 proposes that the public should be made unhappy, and thus subdued by passing laws prohibiting the buying or selling of alcoholic beverages and against public drunkenness.

Many of the most troubling Protocols were adopted by right-wing politicians of their day as a means of motivating their most ardent supporters. By selecting the elements that best served their needs and loading them on the always-rolling anti-Semitic bandwagon, everyone including Adolf Hitler claimed The Protocols were authentic. They became a treasure-trove of rationales for racists.

"We shall destroy among the masses the importance of the family and its educational values," Protocol No. 10 declared.

No. 12 promised, "We shall saddle and bridle the press with a tight curb... Not a single announcement will reach the public without our control."

To tighten the thumbscrews a little more, Protocol No. 14 proclaimed, "It will be undesirable for us that there should exist any other religion than ours...We must therefore sweep away all other forms of belief."

In the economic and political chaos that followed World War One and the Russian revolution, it took only the briefest of references to The Protocols for much of American and European popular culture to seize on them as proof of a secret cabal Jews plotting to take over the world.

Among the advocates was automotive magnate Henry Ford, as previously mentioned, when he launched the Dearborn Independent newspaper in 1920 partially as a means of disseminating The Protocols.

Besides Hitler quoting The Protocols in Mein Kampf, and selections from the book were being read in the Romanian parliament as a rationale for expelling Jews from that country.

16 The Twenty-Four Protocols

The twenty-four Protocols of the Elders of Zion outline how the Jews will dominate the world.

The following is an outline of the twenty-four Protocols:

Protocol I: The Basic Doctrine
Protocol II: Economic Wars
Protocol III: Methods of Conquest
Protocol IV: Materialism Replaces Religion
Protocol V: Despotism and Modern Progress
Protocol VI: Take-over Techniques
Protocol VII: Endless World-Wide Wars
Protocol VIII: Provisional Government
Protocol IX: Re-education of the Masses
Protocol X: Preparing for Power
Protocol XI: The Totalitarian State
Protocol XII: Control of the Press
Protocol XIII: Distractions
Protocol XIV: Assault on Religion
Protocol XV: Ruthless Suppression
Protocol XVI: Brainwashing the Masses
Protocol XVII: Abuse of Authority
Protocol XVIII: Arrest of Opponents
Protocol XIX: Rulers and People
Protocols XX: Financial Programs - Control of the Money Supply
Protocols XXI: Loans and Credit - Enslavement through Debt

Protocols XXII: The Power of Gold
Protocols XXIII: Instilling Obedience
Protocols XXIV: Qualities of the Ruler

ABOUT THE AUTHOR

Ian Day was born in Australia. He lives with his wife, two children, and three cats on his 35-acre ranch, Rancho Diablo, in Arizona.

Made in United States
Orlando, FL
21 September 2023

37134668R00022